CELEBRATING THE NAME AMIR

Celebrating the Name Amir

Walter the Educator

Silent King Books

SILENT KING BOOKS

SKB

Copyright © 2024 by Walter the Educator

All rights reserved. No part of this book may be reproduced in any manner whatsoever without written permission except in the case of brief quotations embodied in critical articles and reviews.

First Printing, 2024

Disclaimer
This book is a literary work; poems are not about specific persons, locations, situations, and/or circumstances unless mentioned in a historical context. This book is for entertainment and informational purposes only. The author and publisher offer this information without warranties expressed or implied. No matter the grounds, neither the author nor the publisher will be accountable for any losses, injuries, or other damages caused by the reader's use of this book. The use of this book acknowledges an understanding and acceptance of this disclaimer.

dedicated to everyone with the first name of Amir

AMIR

In every wave upon the shore,

AMIR

In every breeze that whispers more,

AMIR

Amir's presence gently flows,

AMIR

In every heart, his essence grows.

AMIR

Through life's great dance, through every phase,

AMIR

Through nights of stars and bright sun's rays,

AMIR

Amir, a constant, guiding light,

AMIR

A beacon in the darkest night.

AMIR

His name, a song that ever plays,

AMIR

In forests deep and sunny bays,

AMIR

A melody that stirs the soul,

AMIR

A story written whole by whole.

AMIR

He speaks with wisdom, clear and bright,

AMIR

A voice that turns the wrong to right,

AMIR

In every word, in every deed,

AMIR

A champion for those in need.

AMIR

In every garden, every field,

AMIR

In every harvest that they yield,

AMIR

Amir's spirit nurtures growth,

AMIR

A testament to love's true oath.

AMIR

Through ages past and futures yet,

AMIR

In memories we can't forget,

AMIR

His name will echo, pure and clear,

AMIR

A legacy that we hold dear.

AMIR

In whispers of the morning mist,

AMIR

In sunlight's gentle, golden kiss,

AMIR

Amir, a name that stands alone,

AMIR

A monument of love, stone by stone.

AMIR

In every heart, in every mind,

AMIR

A symbol of the most refined,

AMIR

His name, a beacon, shining bright,

AMIR

A constant source of love and light.

AMIR

So let us celebrate this name,

AMIR

With joy and reverence, acclaim,

AMIR

For Amir's presence in our lives,

AMIR

A gift that evermore survives.

AMIR

In every dawn, in every dusk,

AMIR

In every leaf and tree and husk,

AMIR

Amir, the name that we hold dear,

AMIR

A symbol of the love we share.

AMIR

ABOUT THE CREATOR

Walter the Educator is one of the pseudonyms for Walter Anderson. Formally educated in Chemistry, Business, and Education, he is an educator, an author, a diverse entrepreneur, and he is the son of a disabled war veteran. "Walter the Educator" shares his time between educating and creating. He holds interests and owns several creative projects that entertain, enlighten, enhance, and educate, hoping to inspire and motivate you.

Follow, find new works, and stay up to date
with Walter the Educator™
at WaltertheEducator.com

Milton Keynes UK
Ingram Content Group UK Ltd.
UKHW021950210624
444498UK00015B/357